THINGS I DIDN'T DO WITH THIS BODY

THINGS
I DIDN'T DO
WITH THIS
BODY

AMANDA GUNN

COPPER CANYON PRESS

PORT TOWNSEND, WASHINGTON

Cover art: Sungi Mlengeya, *Dance,* 2021. Acrylic on canvas, 150 × 140 cm.
Courtesy of Afriart Gallery.

Copper Canyon Press is in residence at Fort Worden State Park in Port
Townsend, Washington, under the auspices of Centrum. Centrum is a
gathering place for artists and creative thinkers from around the world,
students of all ages and backgrounds, and audiences seeking extraordinary
cultural enrichment.

LIBRARY OF CONGRESS CATALOGING-IN-PUBLICATION DATA
Names: Gunn, Amanda, author.
Title: Things I didn't do with this body / Amanda Gunn.
Other titles: Things I did not do with this body
Description: Port Townsend, Washington : Copper Canyon Press, [2023] |
    Summary: "A collection of poems by Amanda Gunn"—Provided by publisher.
Identifiers: LCCN 2022045923 (print) | LCCN 2022045924 (ebook) |
    ISBN 9781556596582 (paperback) | ISBN 9781619322714 (epub)
Subjects: LCGFT: Poetry.
Classification: LCC PS3607.U54765 T48 2023 (print) |
    LCC PS3607.U54765 (ebook) | DDC 811/.6—dc23/eng/20220928
LC record available at https://lccn.loc.gov/2022045923
LC ebook record available at https://lccn.loc.gov/2022045924

9 8 7 6 5 4 3 2 FIRST PRINTING

COPPER CANYON PRESS
Post Office Box 271
Port Townsend, Washington 98368
www.coppercanyonpress.org

MIX
Paper from
responsible sources
FSC® C011935

To Linda, my mother, for the conversation of my life

CONTENTS

I

II

III

viii

THINGS
I DIDN'T DO
WITH THIS
BODY

I

FATHER AT TABLE

There was what he demanded with one word
and a pointing finger—"chicken," "cornbread,"
"'tatoes"—the delicacies his labor both purchased
and prepared for us, all his long hours ours. Trying
not to interrupt the table talk that had snapped
shut and refused him. Not vain, not white folk,
he asked only one courtesy: no swearing
he could hear. He was a Christian and my father.
That godforsaken finger. How stingy it seemed
then. Now how tender, how pleading. How I bristled
at the soft of his voice, an engine rumbling under
the hood of our attention. And, oh, what kindness
I held back, expecting things he would never ask
of me: wait your turn, say thank you, say please.

HIGHWAY

What brings us here can barely be called
      highway: a thread of road each direction
and vines overtaking the verge.

      This isn't a dream. Dad
is driving now. We find, at the end of the path,
      three towns where my father

was someone else once. Houses the hue
      of dust and sunflowers that lean in the swelter.
At the Florence Sonic Burger, you'll get a Coke

      for your church program. There are
no mountains in our midst, just twenty-three
      Churches of Christ. This is

the land in which they are grown. This is
      the land in which he was grown, before
something sent him searching. Was it

      my mother waiting unknown, was it
the pulpit he couldn't preach from,
      was it a mask of his own face speaking—

a foreigner from up north?

"A LONG WAYS FROM HOME"

My mother's father never knew his father,
but mornings he could see, as he would shave,
the bluer eyes and there, beneath the lather,
skin paler than his own. His mother gave
her son what start she could from washwork—no,
she wouldn't name the man she'd met or where—
in love or something darker. Not to know
that history bred a rage he seemed to wear.
He wandered far afield, from home to war,
to work, to marriage, out of marriage, gone.
He left the girls his cheerful wife had borne,
still looking for a father, finding none.
In summer he slept days and woke by night,
humming "Motherless Child" in the meager light.

MONARCH

Of Grandma Jessie, little's left: a hymn,
her words like *hootie-rah!* for heat, a gold-
and-rhinestone fritillary pin, grown dim,
a Bible bound with threads too thin to hold.
Her husband left young, his intellect a fire—
he burned. He called her "country": sweet, but cold.
Released, alone, she fixed to her attire
butterflies whose pearls seemed to flash, unmold.
That flat, unpeopled land is still the scene
through which her favored monarchs fold, unfold
themselves from north and home to glorious sun,
their wings cathedral glass, unfettered, bold.
Our Jessie saw them, knew her kin and kind,
and, seeing, lifted skyward in her mind.

GIRL

A girl among boys is most ways alone. My brothers were mean, then sweet, then packed and gone. Mom was looking sideways at how I'd grown—my hair down my neck, my shorts too short. *Too* fast, *too* grown. She had hands that worked. Dungarees. Cotton shirts. Not ruffled or pleated or flounced or flirty, and ofttimes a little bit dirty. She kept house. And quiet and small and tenacious as a mouse, she kept us: three kids, a dog, and a man. She made dinner and Christmas and plans and clothes. I don't think she ever said *No*. More like an *Oh*. A sniff. So, I somehow lost my girlier gear, those things she called prissy: feathered hair, big hoops swinging. Years later she said she hadn't meant to be tough. Her mother had been the salt of the earth. Cleaned nights at Mercy, though she'd sneak a spray of Oscar de la Renta on a holiday or for her Sunday best. Dressed clean for the Lord. Clean for his glory. Her mother before had gone to church and cooked the meals. Nothing less, but never more. What could I do but follow their ways, these sturdy women who'd brought me forth? Even now, the catch of getting out my door is lipstick on, then lipstick off, and bright blouse on, then something plain, asking, *Can I be this thing?* The kind of woman with night-blue lips who's flashing, perhaps, a gaudy ring? Fine thing, being grown. So I step out in ways that can't be seen, a liner-and-lip-gloss subtle sheen and, like my grandma, perfume that *poof!* like a dandelion puff, disappears into eternity. This femme I am, to whom I'm lost and held

and bound, she's cloaked in vapors, reading and
scribbling deep in her papers, doing as someone
would want her to do. *So when—when for Dolly's
lamé-wearing, high-heeled sake—do I get to begin?*
This thing I wear that looks like grace or reserve
or taste but sits on my skin like a stain or a sin,
this thing I bear but cannot name, it may be
this—a borrowed shame.

AFTER SURGERY

She wasn't dying, except
abstractly, my mother,
just replacing each case
of bone on bone until
one by one her joints
were titanium. My brother
and I told jokes across
the hospital bed, made her
laugh her flutelike laugh,
played sound bites
of the bionic woman
leaping felled trees.
Later, light burning
the windows, she sat, small
as death in her chair, whispering,
Mercy, so in pain
she cried tears without
wiping them. My brother
fetched ice. I mustered
the nurses. My father
bent his head toward
his lap, soothing himself
with cooing sounds. How
diminished he, too, seemed,
an old man who
loved her, who could do
nothing, his mind
as shut as an egg.

TO KATI, WHO DOESN'T REMEMBER

Such sounds. Your mother in the kitchen
over a pot of stuffed cabbage, crying, *Istenem,*
istenem, istenem, and you answering her back,
There is no God God is dead he's dead my brother
is dead. What should I say about your brother
in the attic with a gun? He left you alone as he
had always done. Alone in this winter as cold
as the old country. The new country. Irrelevant,
I come to you. I want to be a witness to
your life. So I hold your knees, brave the bloody
room for his papers, make you sandwiches
you plunk onto your breast for later. I fend off
his ex who comes, limbs manic and eyes wild,
into a house we've just got quiet. I stay so
many days. I think, until you can answer
the phone, the door, me, until you can sit
beside his chair, until you can throw out
his glass of whiskey. Until you don't need
the whiskey. I don't know what keeps me
there, past politeness, when my family
says, *Come home, it's Christmas,* when you try
to send me away and your mother nods.
I don't know how so serenely I bear
your rage, shivering and crystalline
in the air between us, though it's mostly
meant for Peter and your own self.
Because you didn't wake at the crack of his .22.
I love you, I say. *You would do it for me,*
I say. This is what old lovers do. Eight years
ago in summer, riding shotgun in your rust-
built truck, I was wrung, sad, unequal
to the heart in my chest, and weary of
the sunlight lifting the maple trees. I wanted

to be gone—a pale and bloody effacement—
as free as Peter would be. Forgive me
for ever feeling I could leave you that way.

SHELLS

Had you known the stakes of winning
that particular argument with your daughter—
it was so small, really.
You couldn't possibly remember it now.
You couldn't have carried it
even into sleep that night.
She stood beside the mop cabinet holding her elbow.
You sat at the kitchen table cracking nuts.
She said something like,
When I talk to you, you just blow me out of the water.
You didn't pause—that was part of it.
Smooth, you like to say, as a gravy sandwich,
you said, *Well, maybe you shouldn't be in the water.*
She was eleven years old,
too old to measure her worship with the span of her arms,
to say, *I love you* this *much,*
but still aching to.
Had you known the stakes of winning that argument
were that, for the rest of your lives,
each time you entered the room her stomach would clench,
I feel certain you wouldn't have cocked a smile
when you spoke.
I feel certain you'd have bitten down
on what felt cleverest,
on what comforted the parts of you your parents shamed.
Though it would have tasted bitter as your pecan shells,
you would have swallowed those satisfactions.
I think you loved her.
I think you loved her that much.

MY FATHER SPEAKS

i

His brother Lafayette
died at the creek
with six boys
standing round him.

My mother told me
these things. Neither of us
knows anything
for certain.

ii

In school in Connecticut
the other Black children
mocked me for the way
I spoke (wannabe-white-girl-
Oreo-cookie). I could hear
North Carolina, Georgia
in their voices, the journey
from South to North
that our parents, grandparents
had taken. I lived
in a white neighborhood.
They thought I spoke
like my neighbors. Each time
I opened my mouth, how
those children must have believed
I hated them.
   Then
they shunned me and I did.

iii

My father is a talking man
and speaks as though
he loves the taste
of his words. He says "purdy,"
as in "purdy as a pan
of buttermilk biscuits,"
which I am
and am told regularly. When I
point this out to him,
this word of home,
he says the word "pretty"
so many times that I begin
to forget who he is. I hope
I am never pretty.

iv

We go back home. There are
yellow brick and dust and clay
I think belong to me.
We play kickball on Christmas Day
and my sneakers redden
in the mud. When I speak,
my cousins call me *white girl.*
They laugh when I say "y'all."

v

I learned to speak from my father.

vi

The year he desegregated
the university, my father

wore silence wherever
he went. Some wished
it would be
his death shroud.
                    The voices
came at night
on the telephone, threatening
a brick against his head or
buckshot to his gut, his father
to be turned out
of the metal factory,
his mother's house to be
brought to kindling.
                    There was one
white girl who smiled
at him each day on his way
to the library. If he had dared
to speak to her, he
would have begged:
Do not be kind to me.
He could feel his starched
collar tight, hear rope
creaking against pine.

vii

Dad, burden me. Tell me the story of how
you found rest at night. Tell me, did the governor

stand at the gate—as he threatened
to? Did your father gaze through the window

into the long evening?

Tell me about Lafayette and what it meant when
we hung a wreath on the door

that Christmas. Tell me about the night you left
for Chicago, never to come back

except on holiday. Burden me with your secret voice.
Tell me about your mother and the restaurant

that went under when they let her go.

LOOK

Knowing Emmett Till had been born
in '41 and my father in '42,

knowing Mississippi made a wound of his only body
while my father's slept tender in Alabama,

knowing how quick my father was to whistle,
to hum, to quip back, to be smart—while Black—

I turned my head in the classroom,
turned my head from the film-lit photograph,

from the misshapen yield of that river,
toward the gentle vacancies of the baseball field.

Oh, child. It's 1992.
Your father will be beside you at the dinner table.

There is a mother whose son was lost to Mississippi.
She's telling you, *Look*.

II

ARAMINTA

Before General, before Moses or Harriet, she was
called Minty. *Araminta:* A name of two roots.
Arabella "yields to prayer." Aminta "defends."
And, oh, where ends the might of that arm?
Perhaps her mama, Rit, felt the squeeze of Minty's fist.
Did she know then her child would wander
from the farm? That she would peer into the marsh
and find the face of God, be blinded one day
in the Philadelphia sun? She arrived
in the new world, new city, crated in pine, a burlap sack
unfurled on her body, wrapped tight under leek
and turnip—coffined, confined, taking each squeak
of the wheel as a sign, each noise she heard as a dog
or a man. Trying to mask her human breath,
the stench of sweat on her human skin. At Combahee
River there were those whose limbs spread upward
in liberation. They crossed the fields, lifting
as in flight, as in a murmuration, as if
moving as one black body against the wind.
Women jostling babies, packets of bread and fat,
grasping chickens, grasping pots still hot with rice;
their men dragging pigs and kids, and kids on thin limbs
catching up or being caught, where alligators snapped
as the maw of the shackle. The overseers running
full tilt on a tackle, as in football, as in sport. The sly
boats whistled, come from the fort, signaling:
we are here, you seven hundred fifty-six, you shall not
be left to the Confederacy. Out front, Harriet
singing a hymn or a lullaby, like church, like bedtime,
a rescue, a soothing. She knew as a girl that those
sold south will march there in coffles, drag chain
for miles. Deep South. Soph and Linah,
Mariah, her sisters—gone. The horizon both

endless and disappearing. Forever out of sight
and hearing and her very capable hands. So she sang
her plans to "master" as she passed him: *Goodbye,*
I'll meet you in the kingdom. And she bowed as if
in deference, as if going about work, and, missing
her reference, he gave a grimace, a smirk. He thought
her faithful, but dim, off-keeled—just good enough
for the work of his field. He did not know her meaning,
her will, her fist, her fox, her game, her would-not-yield,
her God, her faith, her uppity, her name.

THIRTY-NINE OBJECTS
AT THE SMITHSONIAN

and now your face on the dollar you dared
to subvert, covertly moving in the marsh,
mud slalom, old boots or none, guns and fire
and nigger I'm coming for you nigger I'll have
your black hide nigger I'll bleed you like a pig
nigger. Sister, sister. I meditated you here
from a pillow, white cotton and soft. I brought it
back to the breath and the breath brought me you,
my mind unrested. What doubts tested you?
How did you walk into that first night in the dark,
knee-deep through the murmuring creek, the stars
cloaked in cloud and your fellows' fear,
a stack of bills the prize for your fragile, dear throat?
Bills weighed against your body on God's
damnèd scales. Memory fails. I recall just
three things from the tongue my lover taught me,
three things her love bought me—*hello,
I love you, how much does it cost?* What did having,
holding cost, leaving him there, too? How many
twenties would've bought you? How many twenties
to sell you south, rebirth you in the mouth
of America? They called you Minty back then.
Mint leaves scenting the dooryard. Mint jelly
for "master's" lamb. A mint he made off your
goodstrong back, goodstrong teeth, golden,
fresh wheat in your goodstrong hands.
Yesterday I gave away a twenty on the street,
a Jackson, an accident of birth in my pocket,
and the woman's face like a torch caught light.
I turned my head, still and always insufficient
to the day, shamed to have praised
my own self. Oh, Harriet, woman most

equal to your time, you hover there above
my hewn-fine desk, dark, deadly, dead and alive,
knife-keen and waiting and resolute, not
knowing me or needing me, just wanting,
perhaps, that war-pension raise, that cool
twenty you were promised from the House.

MYSTIC

A two-pound weight, hurled toward the sky,
meant to break another, found Harriet Tubman,
collided with her skull at the dry goods store.
Harriet, a hairbreadth from no more—from the end
of her. It splintered bone, that iron stone, barely bigger
than an egg or babyfoot. So put, it drove the fabric
of her head rag home, deep enough to touch her mind.
A madness. Not a man to be kind, her enslaver
would say, *Not worth a sixpence.* She was just
thirteen and, thereafter, she'd feel starlight descending,
the herald of a voice like a bell or a chime.
A slumber would take her then, even as she spoke,
though she woke again, wounded and weary,
breathing and seeing long into time. Crossing, often,
a Manhattan street, without the protection
of the throng, without so much as a turn of my head,
fool girl I was, just wishing herself dead, erased
by a taxi at fifty miles an hour. A dare without
dread, though no small power, I'd dared myself
since thirteen or so. To go and go now: a madness of
my own. No cataclysmic crash on the side of my skull,
just the want of a pill, just chemistry, and thoughts that
moved through me in metaphor. A door to close
or not, as I chose. Harriet and her crew of renegades,
they'd march close, in nothing but rags, rags mocking
clothes. They stepped into the blessèd black and
wicked frost, the stars blue-flaming the waters
they'd wade. Always a river to be followed or crossed,
though there was no promise of blanket or barn or bed.
Just God telling her, *Go and go now,* from inside
her head. Among the night blooms and night birds.
I had a madwoman to disarm, a dweller in my attic
with a shotgun on her arm and a way with her words.

Araminta—African lady, with eyes that pierce the mist—
you yield to prayer and to a voice and to a godly pain.
The price you paid for having no choice. The price
of the railroad with a flesh-made train.
Moses, they'd say, *Moses got the charm.*

CODA: REFUGE

You gaze at me from above my desk,
unsmiling, eyes daring me, well met
by the lens and fixed. Vexed,
you seem, at standing still. Your body
so small in the jaw of the world—
shoulders pressed forward into
labor's cast. Quiet and radical and fast.
Fisher of men. Thief. Spy. Most faithless
slave, most faithful sister. It's a refuge
now, the swamp where you were forced
to plan. And hide and wait. Freeze
and scrounge. Shit and ache and say
goodbye. And travel light. Out
Bestpitch Road, I stand on a bridge,
above still waters that you knew well,
a thick and weedy, fecund hell. A day-
rose moon outshines my face. Weedy
creepers, waters deeper than these boots,
and odors whipping clean away all traces
of my fine perfumes. What blessing
would I have asked back then—
of this refuge, of this both safe
and hostile place? A dryish space
to tuck my head. To rest my bones
as long as the dead.

GO NORTH

Picture yourself at the bus station,
the sun on the brick of the bank.
Imagine real dollars in your pocket,
a woolen coat. A satchel full of
chicken and pound cake. A slide
rule cased in leather. Your mother
stands at your back, your Bible
still in her handbag. Head tilted as
if to say she knows. As if to say: a
mother's duty is to be disappointed.
Don't worry. Her sister will still
meet you in Chicago and show
you where to find warmer shoes.
You wouldn't believe me if I told
you about the cold, how the air
will crack and blacken over a park
bench at night. Would it matter?
You will find work. You will meet
a woman. You will linger some days
in the doorlight of a church. You
will make yourself nearly whole.

NOTES ON A DREAM OF DYING

I know this dream like the lines of my hand.
A spark, unplanned—what I see and see again,
though I wasn't there—his hand, Zaki's, on the door
of the car, his eyes, his face erased by flame.
A scream, a breath. Death piercing the oil tanker,
death holding his legs, death staying his brothers'
footsteps on the bright highway. My cousin Chiquita,
well loved by me, who fed me the caramel cake of our
grandmothers, who told me tidbits of tales, who tipped
her secret ring into the greens, and smiled at me
(at each of us, each) like her very favorite, she lurched
forward, spat blood. A flood came out of her that minute
and, in it, all she'd ever bear or speak or give. I live.
I try to make her recipes. What of Zaki lives in me?
Six months we hadn't called. I, him—he, me.
And, too, I'd passed his place on Bleecker Street.
No hello, no window glance. Just chance, I fixed
my mind that day to set him free. Three days
he'd been dead. How could I not know? This boy who,
years ago, I'd hoped to see again some
short time hence: his heart unfenced, his cheek
in reach, his hand on my shoulder. Me, bolder.
I'm forty. He's forever twenty-two, his face
ice-blue (or ice-black, in fire). He was the first in death
I ever knew, or thought I knew. Though years
before, my mother gave her mother up
harder than this. And for months after, she'd look
beyond me to some further space, to some unpresent face—
Grandma Jessie. God left her as she passed, in terror
of the devil on her last lucid day. The way she had
of walking with death: that Book in her hand, its
moon-dangling, star-spangling lunacy. Mom cursed
the slippery bliss that Jessie sought in God. She was

Jessie's daughter at Jessie's side unseen—unseen
and unknown. I didn't understand until Zaki was gone
why she, my mother, couldn't look me in my eye,
my final bastion on short-term loan, my empty
lunar lake, my lost, last home.

ORDINARY SUGAR

Aunt Mary made graham
cracker cake without
measuring cups, divided
one pound light
brown sugar with a knife,
half for the cake and half
for the pearlescent
hand-beaten, double-boiled
icing. Aunt Earline made
yellow cake with frosting
of real fudge—234 degrees
and all, slow cooled, poured
just before the rapid and
irrevocable hardening.
Ordinary sugar coaxed
to its epiphany.

An heir to their confectionery
sleight of hand, I keep
their notes pressed in a book
and safe. Sugar is poison
to my arthritic knees,
but their recipes will rest,
nonetheless, pristine,
not spoiled with things that
just seem sweet. I'll make
savory dishes out of what
grows green, what snaps
pleasurably, what must,
after twice the loss
of such women, be plenty.

Of Grandma Mattie, sugar
alchemist, it is said, if they
were all she had to hand,
she could make sweet potato
pie out of russets. Seduce
their pale starches until they
tumbled into caramel.
What the loving living tell.
I remember her gleaming
glass eye, her pregnant
wordlessness, her spinning
through the kitchen hot
and fast. Too, the ruthless
manic canning, putting by,
putting by, against memories
too near starvation—the
machine in her belly built
to last. I do not have preserved
in my book how she seasoned
her pear chow-chow or trapped
the summer gardens her labors
made lush. I know only that
she fed the earth her eggshells
and morning coffee grounds,
that she harvested continually
and in fullness, the tender skins
near breaking, near sugar,
always before the chill. Not one
bite lost. She'd mastered,
in a life, how to grow
a winter meal, to till, to weed,
to water, to tend, learned how,
I hope, to be satisfied.

Help me, Lord, to be satisfied.
I was born impatient, under
a vibrating star. But my mother
taught me gently, before
it ached us both to stand,
how to slice fat into cold flour,
sprinkle ice water by tablespoons,
form a perfect discus of dough
without touching it. Unfurl
the crust from a good
French pin. Brush with milk.
A proper flute. Taught me,
too, how to discern and sort
and sugar down the fruit,
and when to fill the plate,
and when to wait, instead,
for the juice to come in.

HYSTERSISTERS

Have I not had my fill of you, dream babies?
You pull fluid from my body in a viscous river,
a red and wholesome, fulsome flood. I cramp and
I shiver. I deliver you (what I have of you) to the
tissue in my hand, to the filthiest waters beneath
dry land. And though this, your egg, is never seen again,
I catch you dreamwise, where you swell inside me
like sacs of butterflies or like that ". . . Lovely" song
by Mr. Wonder or else like the words *I miss you.*
Or like cathedral bells. My never-made bed, my
glassy wish, my gazed-on stars, some light-years away,
already vanished, I have come to let you go. I have
waited like a lover beneath the moon, my feet
in the snow, half sad clown/half loon and, being so,
I have come no closer to your conception. One exception.
I lied to my mother in the doorway in the dark, so I
could fool around with that boy in my room.
Weeks later, alone with a little white stick, my
heart icy-sick, palms slick, I was swearing to the air
I would bring you to an end. Then this morning on
YouTube a giraffe gave birth, pacing her pen
and hoofing the earth. I found myself breathless,
watching her move. She knew precisely what she
had to do, her belly swollen, her body whole—
mine, too. Now I wait for the doctor with my pants
sloughed off, weakly wondering at my mother's line,
and I whisper to myself, *It's okay, it's fine.*
Here's this: I have read hystersisters.com and traced
each algorithm under my palm. He can take this womb.
This brittle, life-torn, Goddess-built flesh, this never-was,
might-have-been locus of rest. He can take what I
have pictured in the quiet meantime—your clenched
brown fists, your serious brow, your sour-milk skin,

39

your tiny will—if a cancer dwells here to crush
and to kill—in me, who never made use of this thing,
who wears neither watch nor diamond ring.

REPAIR WORK

i

We collected in the common room,
eyes moored with sleep, weighed down
with the new chemicals, each of us off
our dark night. Trying to understand
how to wake into a morning we didn't
want to come. They lined us up thrice.
Once for pills, once for vital signs,
once for applesauce and wet pancakes.
Over breakfast and a cigarette break
and coloring-book therapy, we began
to see one another through the stories
we bore. The cocaine addict who awoke
naked and shaking in the road, the alcoholic
left stumbling on the doorstep by his son,
the suicidal one—though weren't we
all that—still sucking charcoal out of
her teeth. By noon I sat with the others,
watching CNN on TV, thinking with some
relief that the election no longer applied
to me, that I wouldn't have to choose,
that I would be gone. I was the one who
had vomited the charcoal, though next
time that measure could be avoided.
And then I would never have to choose
anything again. Then a young man
came toward me in a green hospital
jacket, handsome, bearded, his blue-black
hair sliding sideways with a studied
sweep of his head. He made his way down
the long corridor to where I sat curled like
a pill bug in my armchair. And when he

reached me, I smiled at him, fluttering,
actually fluttering, petal open, as if he
had caught my eye in the subway. He
smiled back, then he handed me a cup
to pee in, and said to drop it at the front
desk when I was done. The blood of desire
and embarrassment suffusing my skin
shifted a thing in me as no pill could
have done. It was the first burden to
return to me, shame, moving under me
like tectonic plates under the landscape.

ii

We came to have our favorites
among the staff, though it was slim
pickings, the way most of them looked
at us. Like handlers at a zoo. Occasionally
affectionate, always wary. Jim was mine.
He gave us two-cigarette breaks and
one-armed hugs, forbidden even when
we cried so hard our toes were clenched
and snot came pouring in rivers out of us.
We told him one night over the popsicles
he'd sneaked us that we liked him most.
He said, *It's nothing, you know. You're not
that much different than me,* proving that
even to the best of them, we weren't
whole, weren't quite human.

iii

My last night we sat in the common room
waiting for dinner to be wheeled in.
The TV was off for a change and someone

(George, the cocaine addict) was
recounting an outrageous tale involving
the police, some ecstasy, his pet ferret,
and a car full of dancers. It wasn't
group, we weren't spelunking through our
childhoods or learning mindfulness
from a box of raisins. We were gathered
around a table, telling dirty stories just like
people with friends do. Once we laughed—
every one of us, it erupted from our guts
like activated charcoal. It couldn't
be stopped. The nurses and techs
came running when they heard it,
convinced, probably, that we were raving,
outside our minds. Maybe fighting
over the remote. All in all, insufficiently
medicated. They didn't understand
a ward full of laughter, the sound of
fragmented souls repairing themselves.

ADMISSIONS

People expect to keep so much with them
when they come. Cell phones, mouthwash.
They're not prepared to encounter Margaret,
the intake nurse, bearing her list of all they must
strip away for twenty-eight days, leaving only the toothed
mouth of time and their utter nakedness.
I'm just a volunteer who's been more or less
there. I bring them decaf tea, a tuna sandwich.
Consolations for the wait and the imposition
of rules no adult would ever have agreed to
ahead of time. In between trips to the kitchen,
I read the *New Yorker* and study a look of openness.
Eyes lifting regularly, smile not so bright it must
be returned, and repeated offers of objects
to distract from the catastrophe through which
they see things right now—*Magazine?*
I try not to ask what you'd ask at a cocktail
party. No *What do you do for a living?* knowing
how a living can be dissolved in the flood and
how those things don't matter here anyway.
There's only what makes a person that signifies,
the chemicals down in the cells, the tissue
of feeling and memory. I do my best to protect them
from the guard, who shouts when he asks
the twelve-year-old why she cuts, asks the man in
the crushed Armani about his last bender.
How on earth he makes them like him
better than me. They remember his name
when they walk out the door. But I go my way,
the way I think makes sense, under the circumstances.
If there's a mom or dad or spouse or a grown child,
I offer talk in restful tones. *How are* you *doing?*
Because I know no one has asked them that

in a very long time. Then I bring them coffee,
the real stuff, and they tell me things you're not
allowed to say about someone you love.
Still, people expect to keep so much.

COLLECT

for Lauren

I remember the warm earthy molds
of the door, the wood rotting gently
beneath its trinity of windows,
the windows arranged ascendingly.
My grandmother prayed in a hierarchy
of light. Jessie's door stood in charity—
open, it seemed, always. The sun baking
away at its damp, fragrant fibers. Inside,
past the wafting doll-head scent
of the plastic sofa covers, her kitchen.
Its generous, freestanding, white
aluminum larder. Penny tang of rusted
hinges. The contact-papered shelves
unfolding the nutty odors of salted
tinned peanuts, honey-roast almonds,
her Fig Newtons. Powder-dry rice
before the sin of butter. I learned

to breathe in in that house, learned
the urge to call things vanished back
and back. To collect approximations
in capped glass jars. My bedroom
closet, a hidden altar bright and full
to bursting, bears bottles of civet oil
and smoke, glittering golden aldehydes.
Elixir enough for a dozen sprawling lives.
But a well-perfumed friend, wise
in the olfactory and in love, taught me
to spray with economy, to wear scent
as a private pleasure, evident only to
a lover in kissing distance. How else

beside privacy—scent so contained
and quiet you must press your nose
to it—to repel the world's in-built
aromas? Manifold, ready to attach,
so potent they are nearly flesh, nearly
hands, reachful in memory. Needful

of collection. Out beyond the double
back window, the willow and the fat
summer air puffing up its mobile hairs.
Beneath it the kingdom of decades'
worth of dogs, each one with his oily,
indolic fur, bathed in summer dust
and fertilizing the earth with scents
that would survive him. I could smell
their sweet, deep-soaked leavings
at night, on the cusp of sleep, curled up
in a pile of cousins within the porous
walls of the porch. Naps, though, I took
in the cloud of Jessie's bed. The Bible
under the lamp. Ancient pages collapsing
out of its feral, musky leather. The scent
of the onionskin still tart and gratifying.
My body felt as weightless as perfume, my hand
stroking the tight-tucked peach percale sheet.
Smooth, blessèd cool, steeped in her Oscar
de la Renta. A watercolor impression
of talcum powder and tuberose and clove.

PRAYER

Lord let me hand you my burden my body it's yours
what will you do with it
my bones are gone to gravel under weight
I loved her
I loved her body as it
grew broad spilled forward filled in its loosened skin filled in
with newfound weight
we stayed at the bar too late we ate with relish chorizo
syruped with figs
I put my cheek against the fat of her belly it felt
cool I felt light as if I had risen taken
a form yet to be baked
I'd stomached every pill I was asked to take some
filled my gut
with a hunger I couldn't sate so sick
from other pills I halved
or quartered meals
misplaced one hundred nine pounds of weight
women who barely knew me said you're so thin so pretty
so lucky you lost a person
it's so so so so great
she fed my body she loved me as I
grew plump again shed my wrinkled skin slowly like
heartache
my breasts so heavy I thought
they'll burst
my breasts so heavy in her hands
can a body burst I think a body can I've known its juice
pills tricked my brain into a motherhood without fruit
I made milk & I burst
I thought what new thing are you body what
are these droplets in my palm
I thought taste it

I thought maybe you'll remember your mother you must have felt
weightless in her arms she waits
for you to call you hand her your laden days she bears you
she gained baby weight to bear you
she lost weight
her muscles grew slack & weak a woman who knew her well said girl
you're wasting away
my mother said
they took you from me in the hospital you didn't know me
you wouldn't feed
it was our very first grief
don't taste no wait for the real thing the authentic thing I thought
there will be other milks to taste
there will be the sweet fat weight of a child a child
my body then refused to make
it was busy carrying weight
too late too late too late
I ask is this it
is this weightlessness
I am weak in my bones from this weight there is bone
in the milk of my knees O sweet Christ
take half my gut or half my legs or half of what's left of my life
you're holding the knife

IV

THE NAME FOR

This place is a sickness where I don't know the language no this sickness is a place where I don't know the language no that's not lithium is a country where I don't know the language my thoughts aren't my thoughts aren't God what is the word for two things together I touch my fingers together it's not exactly *together* there's this stuffed penguin I sit with him under my what's under your *armpit* he's he feels he & I are *connected* yes I found him in a hot train station last Christmas I mean I'm grown I know I told my friend I had a nephew to buy for I do but he's what what is he he's thirteen now why did I bring up the what is it called toy toy right he's a *penguin* no lithium unhooks no that's not exactly whatever OK it unhooks my brain from my um future what's future no I'm trying to tell you the lithium unhooks unhooks my brain from my brain there's no time to time to wait time no it's I can take the dry eyes & & the thirst & the shitting my brains out & the shaking but it's just that I can't think can't talk & instead of words there's just just just just God what's the name for when something you love is dead no not grief no not loss no not funeral no not forever stop guessing for me just give me a minute I can yes time it's not not what's the name for for it it's it's it's

CHRONIC

which is another word for again which is another word for
relentless let's talk about relentlessness three autumns on a
dimmer switch three pale winters I can't get warm in & three
electric sparkling green springs collapsing into summers hung
loose at the hinges skin waking up once numb now reanimate
& alien bursting with sensation I feel my shoulder jump & I
twist it & I twist it I scratch my palms & the soles of my feet
the itch that can't be reached I wring my hands until they ache
& aching they find something is it relief I need & buy & search
& buy & want & buy & can't bear it until it gets here what's
coming again today there are more perfumes than I will ever
wear standing unsprayed in the perfume closet yes I had to make

a perfume closet now the door slightly ajar & unmoved for
seven months seven months that feel like forty days why hold
back I have been in bed since my last best day I passed a test
drank a beer I sometimes strip the gunk from my teeth never
wear socks socks are hard first pair them up sit down put them
on sitting down is hard my shoes I can slip on from standing
that is to say I only wear shoes I can slip on from standing canvas
pull-ons slipping sideways into ice puddles my toes freezing a
shower per month don't get close let me tell you again don't
get close I'm going back to bed I love you but I'm going back
to bed I remember I loved you but I'm going back to bed &
I'm putting on the space heater don't speak to me unless you are

a space heater this stuffed bear is big enough to hold me I named him Bear because I can't & being held I will hold this stuffed penguin & this weird clay doll my grandfather gave me in the '80s her name is Nancy as in Reagan because my dad worked for the Republicans she is part solid earth part velvet all top-heavy ponderous her eyes closed she looks vaguely dead & I understand precisely how she feels vaguely dead she & the animals can stay with me in bed not the cat he prefers the floor with the clothes & the garbage OK fuck we've come this far let's talk about the garbage I'll tell you what there is in this bed wrappers for Twinkies & Sno Balls & Suzy Q's there is Snapple & Gatorade & SunnyD boxes of lemon crème cookies a collection

of Häagen-Dazs cartons cause that's what they sell at Sarah's there are mood stabilizers antipsychotics carbamazepine lithium risperidone quetiapine clonazepam there is no ziprasidone that one made me comatose there is no gabapentin that one made me slow as in my thoughts felt like tadpoles small & slippery & I was too slow to catch them no nortriptyline or duloxetine they made me want to grow my debt & talk too loud & fuck everything there's also metformin verapamil rizatriptan ondansetron diphenhydramine & cholestyramine because my head hurts & my gut hurts & my sugar's up there are romance novels pink covers with frothy bodices muscles lots of cowboy hats romance novels good ones & bad ones I like the bad ones

IS IT OK

Did the antidepressants make me worse did the antidepressants
make me better enough to make it worth it am I worse am
I lost how is that homeless man any different from me why
should he be /You're/ did they warn you before you gave me
antidepressants is it OK to stop is there such a thing as opposing
antidepressants with mood stabilizers in order to minimize
their negative effects /You're very/ can moods be stabilized can
a person be stabilized is opposition real did antidepressants
make me manic did you make me manic whose idea was this
mine will I always be depressed without antidepressants /You're
very bright/ have I reached a steady state is there enough time
for me to reach a steady state before September when school
starts what will I do if I lose my job where will I go if I lose
my housing is it OK not to shower do I have a disability am
I ill is there a Venn diagram showing the relationship between
conceptions of disability & conceptions of illness am I saying
that right /You're a very bright girl/ I'm 42 will I get better
what's better what's human is it OK to have feelings is it human
to be a rock what about a flood is it OK to cry if it's only a little
is it OK to fuck how many times I mean how many times is too
many how many times is too manic is this about containment is
it OK to watch a television show if it makes me cry how many
times per episode what's the difference between a disability &
an illness is the Venn diagram just one circle or is it two full
circles where one stays the same while the other one gets better
or worse where in the Venn diagram is the word *future* is it
better not to have expectations is there a reasonable expectation
I'll get better /I couldn't say either way but you're a very bright
girl/ are lithium & antipsychotics better than antidepressants
is depression better than mania is diabetes better than mania
will antipsychotics make me better enough to make it worth it

can I change my mind can I change your mind is the diabetes permanent what about the thirst what about the hunger will I get fat more fat

Every weekday of thirteen years a yellow note I've fixed
above my desk looks me in the eye & says

EVERY LETTER
EVERY WORD
EVERY PAGE

admonishment
for a missed missed comma I found at last at the point-
end of an editor's finger perfection is the job description
to which I've signed my born name the taskmasters I serve
Big Pharma my eyes fine-toothed eager to catch as on the
last nap left in my Afro morning comes in with a K-Cup I
take it sweet & milky double bland as in a particle-board
cubicle as in the powder in the account exec's perfume as in
the oatmeal in the hand cream beside my keyboard bland
as in my tasteful purse-sized meds case as in the taupe
metal drawer that keeps it what was my favorite flavor
anyway the taste of a good job is beige my serviceable
bread my saltless butter a good job I hold down even
with a new-med headache even when manic I rock in my
chair when I jabber to myself & my team can hear when
the lithium bends me over into the tiny blue recycling
bin I hold it down even with my hot unmarshaled heart
I manage I find again on my raked copyediting stand
marked-up copy comfortingly tight against new clean
copy comfortingly tight against my arms I find again my
finger moving along x-axes down narrow columns I learn
not to read but to glide my feathered mind across the
dark lake of the page I slug I spot I correct I adhere to
style I am adherent I am compliant I am very very good
& I thank God for the calm sensible pleasures of grammar
every letter every word every page prescient sticky note
that said keep me & keep me here how did it know before

I did that it could hold me down its good job know just
how many years days hours I would spend glancing up
those tidy letters saying forget today the cataclysm of your
body all you have to do is be perfect the simplicity of the
mercy of the thing evening lets out past dark past dinner
I click off my monitor I have delivered my deliverables
every one making some modest part of a devil's case every
one hawking shoddy wares meds that help you walk but
give you cancer a tangle on which my comb declines to
catch & by the time I reach the stairs I'm thinking of
the weekend maybe a long nap a couple of action movies
maybe bake a blueberry pie I can share it in the breakroom
on Monday

BAD ROMANCE

Though I have never thought of myself as needing
defense or security or protection or rescue I run out of
good romance my paperbacks from the '90s already
septuple-read leaving me with e-books instaromance
as uncomplicated as Chicken McNuggets they are
available & cheap delicious (if you like to get it the
way Sue Stoker likes to get it) & downloadable the way
no one intended series on top of series + crossovers +
side novellas + sneak peeks of prewritten sequels self-
edited complete with typos *Securing Sidney Protecting
Caroline Marrying Caroline Protecting Fiona
Protecting Summer Protecting Cheyenne Protecting
Alabama Defending Allye Protecting Alabama's Kids
Protecting the Future Rescuing Casey Rescuing Macie*
they come with guarantees stamped HEA for happily
ever after a talisman against ordinary catastrophe
Susan likes her men hyperbutch & gigantic & eager
to marry & her women infinitesimal clever beautiful
without makeup cool in that they never complain
nothing like me they feel smooth & soft & as real-
like as silicone I take my HEAs straight to bed &
I stay there for months while my mother says hello
says Mandy says I love you says it's Thanksgiving it's
Christmas come to the table now it's Easter put that
device down baby your life is passing you by this is
what being rescued looks like a hand & the refusal of
a hand I roll over on the bed too inert to phone the
doctor I keep to my schedule a novel a day my dose
of obliteration as regular as antipsychotics even their
titles seem machine-pressed if you like one there's a
series read *Protecting* twelve more times one device
× twelve hours × infinite days each warm & snug &
decisionless & safe

GOOD ROMANCE

Nearly two weeks I was in the hospital then fresh out & *One Perfect Rose* was my vined & perfumed latticework gateway my bodice not ripped but slowly tantalizingly untied her cover slick white like a pill & library bound a photoreal rose swooning diagonally across her belly I found her behind a scarlet curtain at Jane Addams Books made a porn joke & the clerk blushed bright she sat unassuming beside *River of Fire Thunder & Roses Dancing on the Wind Petals in the Storm Angel Rogue Shattered Rainbows The Rake and the Reformer & The Diabolical Baron* her story solid-late-'90s the sex medium-hot as satisfying as grocery-store sheet cake what seduced me wasn't sweetness but sickness our hero the Duke handsome tall ill beyond all aid yellow-faced & yellow-eyed his gut in full reverse his chest thinning like a sentence & the accidents spillages that had Mary Jo Putney panning away to the window what could you call them but betrayals betrayals of the flesh though not in flower not in rising & roving but in its withering its frailty its inevitability his gut permeable as my permeated brain & then that Rose that one perfect Rose she held his penis in her hand a soft & feeble animal that man & said body you have committed treasonous acts but hush it's OK I am here whatever you are you are also mine my God my brown-eyed Rose you are decent & you are lush & you are capable save me

LEVEL

as in a standard issue carpenter's level you know the
kind with a pert bubble inside a spirit tube the bubble
bouncing lazily back & forth from edge to edge evil spirit
to evil spirit across a marker of good of even Steven of
at last maybe OK a marker both tiny & impossible this
is me looking for the tiny impossible no too manic no
too depressed too depressed & down goes the dose I am
trying to get a bubble into a circle armed with twelve pills
& a charlatan in four and one-half

brisk weeks I buy three
boxes of luxury Japanese facial cotton the big bottle of
Luna Night Oil & when I start on the perfume Guerlain
Samsara & Mugler Aura & Chanel Misia & Chanel
Coromandel & Chanel Égoïste & Chanel No. 5 & even
Aquolina Pink Sugar though what

one person in what right
mind would wear both & then a 1992 vintage bottle of
Guerlain Mitsouko & Guerlain Le Frenchy & Byredo
Pulp & HUM Nutrition Red Carpet supplements built
to make you beautiful from the inside where you are
bloody & tender & your kidneys are already perfect I buy
Dior Miss Dior all six kinds & Dior Dune & Dior Poison
& Dior Dolce Vita & Bella Swan's

entire set of luxury
Italian honeymoon luggage just buff & buttery enough
to be designer my vagina

revving like something engi-
neered & exquisite & German I order the Fun Factory
Boss & the Eroscillator Top Deluxe Soft Finger Combo
Featuring Extra Power & the Tantus Cush & the
Lovehoney Beaded & the Tantus Echo Vibrating in pearl
white & the Vamp Super Soft & the Spartacus Spiral
& the Godemiche Adam in marbled Gamma Ray as

radioactive & gargantuan as my appetites plus limitless
lube Sliquid Sassy & Liquid Silk & BabeLube & Nature
Lovin' Honey Bear Water-Based & überlube & Good
Clean Love Almost Naked

                      & Oh for Jesus Christ's good
holy sake no more up no more green tea no more
moodboost herbal supplements no more blue light
therapy & not one damned more antidepressant I cannot
make this stop I cannot get to sleep I cannot afford milk
I have got to get the bubble in the circle

WAKE

The last time I will ever see you, you are in a box so small I can't contain the thought of it. Raw-wood pale, sharp-cornered, locked tight as death, its smoothed grains meeting across joints as if hewn of one piece. As if before those last impossible human days, you yourself had found it, a felled tree beside the parkway, hurled it with outlaw joy into your pickup, stripped its bark with the tools you had saved for & worked it with the endmost vigor of your arms. To your wake I have carried your favorite perfume, sneaking it like your palm beneath my blouse—gasoline & leather, fresh violets vanishing, already vanishing from the moment I sprayed them & returning your body to me as they go. I want to be the thing that contains you, though I suspect you cannot be contained. The box that bears your ash bears your photograph. Black & white & bordered, snapped in Kolozsvár. It was before the revolution, before your escape. You were incomprehensibly nineteen, in a moment between daydream & flirtation, your smile on the verge of cocking, the sweet boyish cap of your hair poised to swing.

IT'S LIKE WE—

There's none like her left in the—
The world couldn't contain—
So stupid so stupid so—
When on earth did I think I would—
I tried to—
She refused every single—
She wouldn't let me—
It wasn't her fault that she—
She couldn't put down the—
She couldn't climb her way out of—
& what chance did she have to—
The rooms we spent time in are—
So funny the way that she—
The things that she made with her—
& the garden she planted when—
Her body refused to keep—
I should've sent the perfume that she—
& we never finished watching that—
No one has the time that they—
It's like we—
So stupid so stupid so stupid so—
We don't get to keep every—
Why can't we keep every—
She didn't even know how I—
Where has she—
I let her think all those years I didn't—
I wonder if she got the chance to—
Did she know what was going to—
Why didn't she tell me she—
What did she say when she—
Which language did she speak when she—
Was her mother beside her when—

Did her mother find her like—
Was she sober the day that she—
Did she remember—
She never answered my text about—
I never—
I'll never—

RETURN

second pandemic March I
emerge & because I have burrowed
inside my town
a lone furred creature beneath its earth
I forget the turn for Prospect Street
two blocks from my last therapist
her yellow chair that carpet-perfumed air
that terrible silence
one block from the blush-brick church I turned to after
a church whose oak threshold hesitating I
crossed anyway
inside which one bright heavy Sunday
I wept
I can't even remember what particular grief
Kati was still alive still working
her way out of the world
could it have felt worse than this than her gone
I sobbed
even through hymns sung
too gently to lend me cover
even through a beauty I had never seen
a sermon given by a handsome butch
easeful in her big body & silver-
shot hair
not unlike the woman I will always love
& as we passed The Peace
as I jostled my tasseled clutch my wet
cotton handkerchief
warm strange winter-dry hands reached for me
even then even in the face of this
untidy thing my tears
my human body made manifest
to think of it
to think of being touched

TYRANT

Maybe it's a Thursday,
& I'm coming home to make
you dinner. Your mother's paprikás, drop-
dumplings in salted water.
I'm not a half-bad cook. The chicken
will be almost how you remember it. The way
she taught me at her stove. Half pepper only,
no cream, as if
she were still making shift in Kolozsvár, the fine
leather boot of a tyrant in her teeth.
I understand why you never believed in God.
What on earth could more kneeling
have afforded you?
My faith feels stingy & small.
I only speak
to God
when I have no choice.
Though there are days I feel
as if someone hears me. But I was talking
about a Thursday.
I am laboring up the stoop with an ache
in my back. Maybe my arms
are filled with groceries in paper bags. Maybe each bag
is torn in two places. I lift one as high
as I can into the crook of my arm. Golden onions
tumble to the ground
in the lily of the valley. We cut them
by handfuls in spring. They are early
& pale & sweet like a lover's first question.
Maybe the bags are breaking now.
I manage the lock, the flour dusting
the threshold. & I shout for you as I kick the door
closed with my heel.

Can you grab the bags?
But the kitchen is empty. The house is empty.

NEVER NOW

Queen of the horseradish smear the run-red clouds of
blood & bits of meat Queen of leave the dishes they'll
keep Queen of broken crystal knobs tumbling off the
door Queen of cat hair stuck to golden spills of vomit
on the floor Queen of it's dry already it'll hold Queen of
coffee cold & untopped-up Queen of that same coffee
cup with velvet spots of mold Queen of maybe later
quad sets to rehabilitate my knees Queen of please please
don't ask again Queen of never-when Queen of better yet
leave it off my plate Queen of true love-words discovered
bitter-late Queen of never-said Queen of two ex-lovers
dead Queen of every call I failed to make Queen of worse
the calls I declined to take from her from him Queen of
that day one day I'll mend things with my dad Queen of
future-admit Queen of future-forgive Queen of I need
peace just just for a while Queen of things deferred to
disappearance a yellow house a proper porch a city I
could keep for life a child Queen of I'll sort bills later
leave the boxes by the bin Queen who would delay the
honey-green germ of spring to stop a little snow coming
in Queen of next week is fine it's fine I've made a list I
swear I promise I'll take the car in for repair I'll go Queen
of not-now I'm sorry no

WHAT YOU MEANT

I tell my mother everything that hurts. We disagree
about the night you kicked your leg—
that swollen, leaking leg—against the wall,
thick as the trunk of a tree.
I told her what you meant when you last spoke.

She couldn't understand me at all.
You meant to call them back, my mother said, the ones you loved
and saw inside the light.
She'd lost her mother, now, three decades back. A fact
that I forget.

She was a daughter first, long before we met.

But, love, I think you saw, instead, that summer
by the sea, against the chipped white boardwalk fence,
you three:
Édesanya, Peter, your beanpole preteen self, all younger
than you ever were to me—

skinny, happy, burnt till bittersweet. Your days ahead
still savory, still possible. Lit, too, a rockless, silken beach,

before the clerk X-ed out where you could see
those papers you'd prepared—so eager, so smart, so scared—
for entrance to the special science school.
The single Magyar seat already full. That's it
for the likes of you.

The clever, able self you saw there, too—
first of your family, Édesanya, Peter, puffed and proud.
X-ed out.
Your heart. The life after.

Peterke, you called him. Little brother with that grim
and dashing grin,
that loaded gun. He left you first and fast.

And Édesanya, "sweet mother."
Two months too scared to call, I called at last, I thought
for her sake, anyway.
She knew you well, the bones you had to take.
How you sucked them dry your uncomplaining way.

I knew you, too—the taste of your taste.
The pleasures your ample, precious body
could contain.
I watched you eat your onions cut with salt, the fat
of bacon crisping in your pan
or raw into the mouth, cold and plain.

There was a black and glossy egg you longed to eat.

All those years you were dying—and knowing it—and loving me,
while I was counting bottle caps beside your plate.

And now, as if I've marked you with an X, I want you
to have left the room in peace.
But you kicked the wall. You said, *Wait. Wait.*

KALEIDOSCOPE

The day he learned he likely had cancer
more tests the doctor said my mother said
my father sent his children
a video clip
sound down I clicked through
I don't always
to find a thick kaleidoscope of monarchs
overwintering
in a snug humid Mexican forest
hard to tell at first what odd-
textured fabric weighed down
the branches shrouded
the ancient trunks
then closer it seemed not fabric
but a proliferation of petals
born of the trees & grown
like children
too heavy too many for the trees to carry
then closer closer the minute flexing
no longer petals then
but a looming body of creatures in deft camouflage
together magnificent
tall as a father
every turn of a wing the involuntary trembling
of a pinky finger
every movement shimmying out the monarch's body proper
what I had begun now to long for
a glory of black & flame black & flame
how they released themselves so knowingly
into the soft
wet air black & flame black & flame
fabric again yes transformed by instinct
shredded confettied airborne

every monarch in singular spiral flight he didn't write
a word not
our lives my life my whole life
not even
I love you he just
pasted the video into the frame as if
to say to us his living children
I couldn't keep it to myself these creatures this
impossible joy
this is the most
important thing I could tell you today

BAKER

The pleasure is not
this made, golden-
brown thing, crisp
shell, plump with
currants, pecans
chopped so small
they are equal with
the crumb, the texture
in the jaw soft
as the pad of a thumb.
That is the business
of Christmas-tree
tins & houseguests, ones
I am fond of or not,
but am willing enough
to labor for. Even
love is not the pleasure.
It doesn't sanctify
the chore. The pleasure
is in the perfume. Butter
creamed into sugar
shot through
with molasses, vanilla
striking the salt
inside the butterfat.
The heat of the inner
cinnamon bark
ground until fragrant
& fine, like a palm
of fruitful soil, like
a fortune.
The pleasure is in
kitchen-warmed

eggs, silky, saucing
the dough, in a blue
bowl with heft,
which I purchased
with good money
& which is more
than capable
of containing them.
Even when I take them
by the dozen, even when
I rouse them with
my whisk—
their froth, their
saline animal odors.

SHALIMAR

The new disease came as a surprise to her, like a whiff
of Shalimar. Smoke, iris, bergamot, evening before utter
dark. It turned her bones into gravel. And who were her
old aches to bend before the new? Her knees still throbbed.
Her face still looked like her mother's. And now her living
body gave it succor, the cancer, even at her expense. Each
day she woke, bracing herself for the smaller disasters of
dying. A broken foot, a snapped finger, the Tareytons
she had to give up. She held her Bible and prayed until
morning wore itself thin, through soap operas and mock
judges, through *Wheel of Fortune* and the news. Until
night came again, that miserable smart aleck, cloaked in
vapor, telling her dreams like dirty jokes. What would her
daughters say, when they returned? She could see them
already. Ghostly eyes, gnashing teeth, arms outstretched
with purple blooms.

MORNING AT CRASH BOAT BEACH

I thought I'd die that way—cold in my sunburned
skin, in the sweet unxenial waters of Aguadilla.
Do you remember the last morning we swam off
Crash Boat? Beneath the surface of what was green
and felt infinite, we waggled our limbs. It was
the strength of our legs kept us there, though it
should have been something else. You might have
lifted me into the wave, but I wouldn't let you.
There were lovers whispering when the tide
came in. Then *ta-da!* You asked me why, your eye
fixed on a man with a gull on his hat. What could I say—
that I might never choose you? That night, mouth
cloying with aspartame and whiskey, you said, *Stay.*
You said, *Not yet.* You held my vulva in your palm.

ALL THINGS

Across a distance you're
the one I've wanted, ever.

There're no more plates of fish
to fry, no longer snow

tracked on the floor. I hear
a bottle clink the sink

across the phone and know
I've dreamt this. Is that sound

you, eating onion? Is
your foot beneath the dog?

I like to say I've brought
you here with me, but I

just have a picture: you,
as drowsy, ruddy, loose

as I can ever quite
recall, the obstacle

to what I longed for when
I left you in the fall.

POETIC EXERCISE IN THE SERVICE OF LOVE

after S.X. Rosenstock

Her collar pop, her victory dance, her strut,
her cowboy boots, her bolo tie, and more—
her ragged leather coat that touched the floor.
Her basement bedroom set, her screaming mutts,
her rowdy kin, her constant cracking nuts,
her "baby-girl," her jellied meats, her snore,
her toothy kiss, her soccer-TV roar.
Her beers in bed, her drink, her drunk, but what
could only be called chivalry. And toes:
so fat and cold on tickle-torture nights.
Her velvet hair, her hands that feared no grime,
her Marilyn mole, her take-it-as-it-goes.
Those pizza dates. Her hunger, her delight
in old things, new things, me. Her laugh, her time.

PATIENCE

The animal inside hasn't finished
with me. She's descending her tree.
I won't call her *love*. She's something
more dear, like *need*, like *lack*, an ache
that aches me—just here.
You've never trusted me, said my last
love. She was making our dinner
with me at the stove sneaking in salt,
or was it her hand on the wheel and
my eyes on asphalt, or her hand
on my thigh and my eyes turned—
where? Not knowing, myself, I lied.
I said, *Of course I do*, but did I dare to
or care to? She wanted me swooning,
she took each hesitation as a wound.
And you, my oldest friend, she never
understood you or us. The years
that I've been knowing you, and
still we've never fucked or kissed
or tried and missed. Since our band
that was doomed, since our book club
of two, reading *Zami* and *Patience*
and *Rubyfruit*—thirty years and some.
You knew me back when my
father baked the bacon and the
perfect grits, when he spun Stevie
Wonder and disco in fits, and at
the moment I most wanted him to,
he threw me into the air, and I'd
scare and shriek like a baby goat.
That was the best of him, the high
note. I once asked him: couldn't he
be easy or, at least, less hard?

He said wade in the water, be ready
to drown. I trusted, then, that he
controlled the tide, that he in his
might would wrench me down.
Wordless, I watched him like
a thin-grown fox watches the ocean
as it rushes the beach and the docks,
lifting her paw—is it in question
or in pain? Just when did you
get on this downtown train?
From where did you spring on this
death-rattling earth? With your
seasoning my pan, or your hand
on my wheel or rubbing my shoulder,
hemming me in for all that I'm worth,
with your spinach in every dish,
your brisk winter walks, your hiding
the sugar and making me sleep and
have real talks. *I trust you,* I say.
A prayer that I speak, a prayer I enact,
to be blessed and brave but remain,
somehow, remain intact. You jest,
So skeptical, Gunn! How can I tell you
I was made this way—wary of love
and weary of heart, that I'm unmade
part by part by you? I'm looking
just there at your animal throat,
the fluttering space behind your ear,
the wool of your scarf and the soft
of your coat. The animal inside me
is at it again. She's descending
her tree and slinking her hips and,
ever so lonely, parting her lips.

HOUSEHOLD

for Moon

Ate a sweet fig
we didn't grow,
wanted it
New England
greener,
sliced the eggplant
thinner than
you taught me,
grilled it myself
until it burned.
Walked a mile
to the spice shop
on my bum knee.
Didn't complain.
Tripped my trick
hip, stopped
halfway for soup
and three Tylenol.
Did you proud:
skipped the Thai
iced tea, sugar
addict luxury,
bent, you said,
on worming
my joints. Bought
organic chicken.
Fried it the way
you like but won't,
anymore, let
me make, skipped

the butter biscuits
you always do.
Met an old friend
over pasta, met
a new one over
injera. Invited.
Was accepted.
Was refused.
Was OK, actually.
Told the fresh,
shockingly cold
Berkeley air
in your place,
I manage to leave
my bedroom
most days now.
Most days, I've
learned to do
a thing.
Like trying
Leila's, like visiting
fat botanical
microclimates
without saying
gross or even
thinking it.
Liked, in fact,
the darkest,
thickest one.
Found a proper
queer barber
for your foxy
frosty hair, found
a schnitzel spot

to take you to,
scouted the best
neighborhood
taqueria, tried some
dishes on
the spicy side.
Stocked hot red
pepper, eleven ways.

STORMWATCHING IN CAMPANIA

for my brothers

You could have found us anywhere,
              on the bank of any
          undulating river,

we didn't have to be
              in the shadow
         of someone's volcano,

wine nearby,
              watching lightning
         shatter the upper sky,

olives pelting lazily
              the slate.
         There didn't have to be

lemon trees
              loosed of their fruit,
         nor wisteria

ascending ancient stone.
              We needed only
         each other and to forget

what it meant
              to be weighted,
         grown, distinct,

needed only
              to rest a while
         in pregnant darkness,

our hands empty,
             our eyes absent
        of electronic

white light.

HAPPY AND WELL

i

A better year than most, give
or take, though the world is filled

with so much light it seems
alien: vegetation bluish and hearty,

a landscape with too much sun.
On a Tuesday night in spring

I call my mother—not exactly
not crying:

I think I might be happy.

ii

My aunt and uncle tell jokes in the best way possible—
laughing so hard they can't finish them.

They've spent sixty-five years setting
a common table, praying a common prayer.

My uncle sweeps the kitchen twice a day.
My aunt folds clothes when my uncle annoys her.

The cake she offers me before dinner is the cake
their daughter once made.

She says, *Enjoy it.*

My uncle will hand you a smoked turkey
as you leave for the airport. His masterwork, that barbecue.

This abundance produced three children. The first
when they were just fifteen.

One they lost to a blood clot. One to cancer.
The last to prison, irrevocably.

Sometimes my auntie and uncle sit each to a room. Bodies
still, unable to speak.

Just sometimes.

iii

When we got married, my aunt says, *we decided then to be happy.*

iv

Mania comes dressed as happiness
in gunmetal sequins.

Is she happy today? Or is she manic?

Me at sixteen, trying on a prom dress
much too expensive for us.

I mistake myself for a stranger
in the far mirror.

She looks some kind of sick.

v

My most beautiful friend takes self-portraits for catalogs
and Instagram.

Her curls shine with good genes, quality coconut oil, the absorbing
daily labors of Black hair.

Her climbing muscles pop from her cross-back tank
as she suspends herself from cliffs. The California dust

a rouge on her cheek.

In every single portrait without fail, she laughs
uproariously. Something silent, irrepressible.

I can't look.
Her head always thrown back. Every tooth out as if poised to bite.

vi

There were minutes in the afternoons, insufficient ones,
when my mother would hide in her bathroom

while my brothers and I shrieked and played outside.
Her three babies. The ones who had lived.

She told my grandmother on the phone,
Sometimes—they're just too happy.

She'd spent her whole life making herself a mother.
The house she grew up in she called hell house.

vii

My mother painting yellow tulips again
and again and again on a scrap

of watercolor paper.

When asked, she gives the study to me.
Baffled, amused, granting a gift

she doesn't quite understand.
My new rubric.

On the back I find she has scribbled: *Happy Spring!*

viii

I ask a brother—a particular type of brother—
How are you today, Sir?

He is a pastor and a very fine
shade-tree mechanic,

both of which afford him a certain deference.
He smiles at me, nothing held in reserve,

no joy socked away to himself
for later,

and says, *Happy and well.*

And goddamn he means it.
What must it feel like to mean it?

I think, if he asked me this minute,
I would marry this man.

He says it again.
I feel myself thrown forward,

as if sitting the wrong way on a departing train,
as if riding his open heart from the shadow of the station.

ELEGY

      Drug-softened, sweet
as a tooth
      in decay,
child I didn't,
      won't have—
babykitten grown
      older than me
and dead now.
      Oil-slicked,
fur-warmed soul.
      Creature created low,
boxed out
      of the light
of God
      like so many of us
from our fathers.
      A prayer for you:
find Kati,
      your pagan patron
gourmand saint,
      our just-lost love
something
      couldn't let me
replace, nor,
      while she lived,
let go of.
      She will see you
roughrubbed,
      see you proper
fed, fed
      fine. Kismet:
her hand, open,
      outstretched

toward mine.
      That first
voluptuous-
          petaled bouquet.
      And you,
your fresh wet
          nose, still young,
not yet febrile,
          leading you inexorably out
from self-exile,
          straight to the hem
of her garment.
      Me too.
She led me out
      too.

THINGS I DIDN'T DO WITH THIS BODY
& THINGS I DID

I didn't bear a child with it, bear a drunk friend's arm around its shoulders, bear it over a fence in one go, bear it from Harlem to Wall Street by foot, run it until it vomited, run it until it vibrated with joy, lean it long against a redwood it had hiked to, lay it on the earth beneath the aurora borealis, march it white-laced until it wed, march it in Baltimore for a killed Black man, march it to war until it was dead, bear a lover eager on its spine, bear it back to its natal soil, bear it to the lake's center under the swift awesome power of its legs. Bear witness: I did not make its child. I didn't bear it to the home it asked me for. Instead, as if by stumbling, as if by walking backward even, as if the beginning & not the end held the drum & cymbal & jazz hands,

I bore three lovers in its mouth, bore a blow to its cheek, bore the snap & drag of the Atlantic at high tide, bared its breasts on that beach, scored its ankle with a knife twelve thin times, bored into the white underflesh of its thigh, bore its scars, bore tattoos to cover its scars, bore hot wax where it was tenderest, bore on its face a heavy, pretty face, bore smoke deep in its tissues, bore the soft, bore the love of its family. Withheld from it embraces, withheld from it a decent meal. Bore love for the boy who refused it, bore the death of the boy who didn't, bore the weight it made from the pills I had handed it, bore its joints' irreparable ache, bore the turned, sweet smell beneath its breast, taught water to bear it so I could rest, bore its sloughings, bore its swellings, bore its manifold solitudes, and on the rare, keen nights it stayed with me, I bore its bright fragrant solitary intolerable pleasure.

LIKE THIS

Erykah says *melodies prayers babies*

A woman who isn't asked says nothing

A woman who isn't a mother fields questions

A woman who isn't a mother owns a field

My mother holds my knee

My mother's left hand is a wooden shield

My mother tells her cousin *when she's ready*

A woman who waits—

Erykah says we *give birth to different things*

A woman who knows the difference says *poems*

A mother slices a pepper like a heart

A mother says *like this*

My mother holds a braid holds the milk holds a chrysalis

One mother says *you dodged a bullet*

A woman who waits waits for a sound in her heart

A doctor says what saves you

What saves my life will burst a baby's heart

A doctor says *choose*

My mother's hand in the car hits my heart

A mother's grief arrives already swaddled

A mother with ashes for children says *istenem*

The woman who birthed my mother says *maybe*

A woman who's no longer asked says *nothing?*

Erykah says *birth things*

A woman who makes a choice works a field

My mother taught my hands to crimp the pastry

I taught my mother's hands to lattice pastry

The woman who birthed my mother says prayers

My mother holds a needle holds a feather holds a door

When a doctor says *choose* a death is meted

A poem says the same each time you meet it

A woman who doesn't choose crosses a field

NOTES

The title "A Long Ways from Home" is borrowed from a line in the spiritual "Motherless Child" (traditional).

"My Father Speaks" references the time my father spent at the University of North Alabama, formerly Florence State College. In 1963, with the help of activist and civil rights attorney Fred Gray, he sued to transfer into the then-segregated school and was the first Black student to attend.

The four poems of Part II on Harriet Tubman (the "Wade" series, after the spiritual "Wade in the Water") are indebted to a number of textual sources as well as a site visit I made to the Cambridge, Maryland, area, near Tubman's birthplace. Pertinent texts include Catherine Clinton's *Harriet Tubman: The Road to Freedom* (Back Bay/ Little Brown); early biographer Earl Conrad's archive, housed at the Schomburg Center for Research in Black Culture, New York Public Library; the Fugitive Slave Acts of 1793 and 1850; Lois E. Horton's slim but invaluable *Harriet Tubman and the Fight for Freedom: A Brief History with Documents* (Bedford/St. Martin's); Kate Clifford Larson's *Bound for the Promised Land: Harriet Tubman, Portrait of an American Hero* (Ballantine), and finally William Still's 1872 *The Underground Railroad: A Record of Facts, Authentic Narratives, Letters, &c., Narrating the Hardships, Hair-Breadth Escapes and Death Struggles of the Slaves in Their Efforts for Freedom, As Related by Themselves and Others, or Witnessed by the Author* (Porter & Coates).

The poem "Like This" includes fragments from "Reprise (Live)" by Erykah Badu.

ACKNOWLEDGMENTS

Thank you to the editors of the following publications for publishing these poems, sometimes in earlier versions:

The Adroit Journal: "Thirty-Nine Objects at the Smithsonian"

The Baffler: "Notes on a Dream of Dying"

Birmingham Poetry Review: "Never Now"

Colorado Review: "To Kati, Who Doesn't Remember"

Conjunctions: "Collect," "Highway," "Stormwatching in Campania"

The Cortland Review: "Morning at Crash Boat Beach"

Diode Poetry Journal: "Is It OK"

Harvard Review: "Shalimar"

The Hopkins Review: "Poetic Exercise in the Service of Love"

Kenyon Review: "Bad Romance," "Chronic"

Lana Turner: "Things I Didn't Do with This Body & Things I Did" (reprinted in *The Pushcart Prize XLVI: Best of the Small Presses 2022 Edition*)

Narrative: "Baker," "Kaleidoscope," "Prayer," "Return," "Tyrant"

The Offing: "Happy and Well"

Pensive: "Father at Table," "Repair Work"

Peripheries: "'A Long Ways from Home,'" "Monarch"

Poetry: "Araminta," "Mystic"

Poetry Northwest: "Hystersisters" (as "hystersisters.com"), "Patience"

Redivider: "After Surgery"

Southern Humanities Review: "Araminta" (as "Raid at Combahee River, June 2, 1863"), "My Father Speaks"

32 Poems: "Elegy," "Girl," "Household," "Look"

Tupelo Quarterly: "Good Romance," "Level," "The Name For"

Unsplendid: "All Things"

Thanks to the Writing Seminars at Johns Hopkins University, the Stanford University Creative Writing Program, the Harvard University English Department, and the Kenyon Review Writers Workshop for resources to support this project. Thanks especially to Jorie Graham for her wisdom and mentorship; thanks also to Mary Jo Salter for her teaching and continued support. Thank you to my advisor Glenda Carpio for championing my creative as well as my critical work. My gratitude to the entire wonderful team at Copper Canyon. Thank you to my fellow Hopkins, CAPR, Stegner, Kenyon, and New York State Summer Writers Institute poets. Thank you to Richie Hofmann, Keetje Kuipers, and Natalie Shapero for their generosity over the years. Thank you to my friend and longtime first reader, Lauren Winchester, for her attention, insight, and constancy. Thank you to Moon Duchin for her abiding friendship and love and for her keen eye, especially during the critical final years of this project. Finally, thanks to my family & to dearest Katika—for being my soft place to land, my home.

ABOUT THE AUTHOR

Amanda Gunn is a poet, teacher, and doctoral candidate in English at Harvard where she studies poetry, ephemerality, and Black pleasure. Raised in Connecticut, she worked as a medical copyeditor for thirteen years before earning a master of fine arts degree in poetry from the Writing Seminars at Johns Hopkins. She is a 2021–23 Wallace Stegner Fellow in poetry at Stanford, the inaugural winner of the Auburn Witness Poetry Prize honoring Jake Adam York, the recipient of a writing fellowship from the Civitella Ranieri Foundation, and the recipient of a Pushcart Prize.

Lannan Literary Selections

For two decades Lannan Foundation has supported the publication and distribution of exceptional literary works. Copper Canyon Press gratefully acknowledges their support.

LANNAN LITERARY SELECTIONS 2023

Jaswinder Bolina, *English as a Second Language*

Natalie Eilbert, *Overland*

Amanda Gunn, *Things I Didn't Do with This Body*

Paisley Rekdal, *West: A Translation*

Michael Wiegers (ed.), *A House Called Tomorrow: Fifty Years of Poetry from Copper Canyon Press*

RECENT LANNAN LITERARY SELECTIONS FROM COPPER CANYON PRESS

Chris Abani, *Smoking the Bible*

Mark Bibbins, *13th Balloon*

Jericho Brown, *The Tradition*

Victoria Chang, *Obit*

Victoria Chang, *The Trees Witness Everything*

Leila Chatti, *Deluge*

Shangyang Fang, *Burying the Mountain*

Nicholas Goodly, *Black Swim*

June Jordan, *The Essential June Jordan*

Laura Kasischke, *Lightning Falls in Love*

Deborah Landau, *Soft Targets*

Dana Levin, *Now Do You Know Where You Are*

Philip Metres, *Shrapnel Maps*

Paisley Rekdal, *Nightingale*

Natalie Scenters-Zapico, *Lima :: Limón*

Natalie Shapero, *Popular Longing*

Arthur Sze, *The Glass Constellation: New and Collected Poems*

Fernando Valverde, *America* (translated by Carolyn Forché)

Michael Wasson, *Swallowed Light*

Matthew Zapruder, *Father's Day*

Poetry is vital to language and living. Since 1972, Copper Canyon Press has published extraordinary poetry from around the world to engage the imaginations and intellects of readers, writers, booksellers, librarians, teachers, students, and donors.

WE ARE GRATEFUL FOR THE MAJOR SUPPORT PROVIDED BY:

academy of
american poets

THE PAUL G. ALLEN
FAMILY FOUNDATION

amazon literary
partnership

4
CULTURE

the point
envision·enact·evolve

Lannan

ART WORKS.
National
Endowment
for the Arts
arts.gov

WASHINGTON STATE
ARTS COMMISSION

A&
OFFICE OF ARTS & CULTURE
SEATTLE

The Witter Bynner Foundation
for Poetry

TO LEARN MORE ABOUT UNDERWRITING
COPPER CANYON PRESS TITLES,
PLEASE CALL 360-385-4925 EXT. 103

WE ARE GRATEFUL FOR THE MAJOR SUPPORT PROVIDED BY:

Richard Andrews and Colleen
    Chartier
Anonymous
Jill Baker and Jeffrey Bishop
Anne and Geoffrey Barker
Donna Bellew
Matthew Bellew
Sarah Bird
Will Blythe
John Branch
Diana Broze
Sarah Cavanaugh
Keith Cowan and Linda Walsh
Stephanie Ellis-Smith and
    Douglas Smith
Mimi Gardner Gates
Gull Industries Inc. on behalf of
    William True
The Trust of Warren A. Gummow
William R. Hearst III
Carolyn and Robert Hedin
David and Jane Hibbard
Bruce S. Kahn
Phil Kovacevich and Eric Wechsler
Lakeside Industries Inc. on behalf
    of Jeanne Marie Lee

Maureen Lee and Mark Busto
Peter Lewis and Johanna Turiano
Ellie Mathews and Carl Youngmann
    as The North Press
Larry Mawby and Lois Bahle
Hank and Liesel Meijer
Jack Nicholson
Petunia Charitable Fund and
    adviser Elizabeth Hebert
Madelyn Pitts
Suzanne Rapp and Mark Hamilton
Adam and Lynn Rauch
Emily and Dan Raymond
Joseph C. Roberts
Jill and Bill Ruckelshaus
Cynthia Sears
Kim and Jeff Seely
Nora Hutton Shepard
D.D. Wigley
Joan F. Woods
Barbara and Charles Wright
In honor of C.D. Wright,
    from Forrest Gander
Caleb Young as C. Young Creative
The dedicated interns and faithful
    volunteers of Copper Canyon Press

The pressmark for Copper Canyon Press
suggests entrance, connection, and interaction
while holding at its center
an attentive, dynamic space for poetry.

This book is set in Adobe Garamond and 1786 GLC Fournier Caps.
Book design and composition by Becca Fox Design.
Printed on archival-quality paper.